茉莉之屋：

探寻汉语学习的乐趣

王靓一　著

Jasmine Wang

Jasmine's House

*A place where you could find
the joy of learning Chinese*

中国华侨出版社

· 北京 ·

图书在版编目（CIP）数据

茉莉之屋：探寻汉语学习的乐趣 / 王靓一著 . —北京：中国华侨出版社，2023.1
ISBN 978-7-5113-8914-5

Ⅰ. ①茉… Ⅱ. ①王… Ⅲ. ①汉语—对外汉语教学—学习方法 Ⅳ. ① H195.3

中国版本图书馆 CIP 数据核字（2022）第 190886 号

● **茉莉之屋：探寻汉语学习的乐趣**

著　　者 / 王靓一
责任编辑 / 桑梦娟
封面设计 / 石　芃
经　　销 / 新华书店
开　　本 / 710 毫米 × 1000 毫米　　1/32　　印张 / 5　　字数 / 82 千字
印　　刷 / 三河市中晟雅豪印务有限公司
版　　次 / 2023 年 1 月第 1 版
印　　次 / 2023 年 1 月第 1 次印刷
书　　号 / ISBN 978-7-5113-8914-5
定　　价 / 49.80 元

中国华侨出版社　　北京市朝阳区西坝河东里77号楼底商5号　　邮编：100028
发行部：（010）64443051　　传　真：（010）64439708
网　　址：www.oveaschin.com　　E-mail：oveaschin@sina.com

如发现印装质量问题，影响阅读，请与印刷厂联系调换。

散发着茉莉芬芳的独特雕纹

金翠华

Jin Cuihua

　　先是看到《茉莉之屋——探寻汉语学习的乐趣》的提纲，我宛若看到一座建筑的框架，没有高耸云端的傲情，没有开山劈岭的狂气，更没有占地万亩的贪欲。它坚实的根基，方正的支架，奇妙的造形，让我急于看到小屋的建成。

　　建成了！一座散发着茉莉芬芳的美丽小屋出现在蓝天白云下；在坎坷蜿蜒的人生道路边——不是旅馆，不是观光景点。鲜花盛开的屋门日夜敞开，敞开的屋门流淌出爱的笑语，那笑语如此亲切，如此坦荡，像清澈的溪流洗涤着每一个过路客心灵的疲惫，引领你走进这奇特的小屋。走进小屋，你惊喜地发现小屋宽敞明亮，竟然有八个错落有致的房间，每个房间的门都是敞开的，门前没有任何遮挡。你完全可以任选一个房间看个究竟。但是你没有。你站在小屋中间，上下左右环视着那些散发不同香气的房间，欣赏各房间门板上独特的雕纹以及在雕纹里生长的鲜活的花草虫鸟。是的，你谦卑好学，你知道不论学什么，你的耳、目、鼻、舌、身都要全体出动，才能开拓思维，洞察事物的本质，抓住学习要领，学到最重要的知识，进而在实践中把知识转化为能力。你明白这一点，所以你在认真地观察。你看到每一个房间门板上的图案都不同。那个刻画着变形刀叉碗盘的门上，金色的麦穗儿垂挂在交错的刀叉中；旺盛生长着的翠绿菜蔬把各种变形的盘碟连成一畦畦菜地；每一个变形的碗里都游动着形色各异的鱼虾……太美了！从门里飘出的是各种喷喷香的饭菜气味。你明白了，这个房间展示的是中国食文化。

你的嗅觉把你引到另一间门前。门里飘出的是清雅的芬芳。那芬芳直抵你的肺腑，让你心清气爽。你愉快地拽了一把从雕花门板上抽出的清新的枝条，枝条上长满了柔嫩的绿叶。你掐了一片绿叶，轻轻用手指揉搓，你的手指便沾满了清冽的馨香。你笑了，你知道这个房间展示的是中国的茶文化。

没等你回过神儿来，你的心就被高亢的歌声和铿锵的鼓点儿抓住了。你疾步走近那扇门，这才听清：歌声和鼓点儿不是从门里冲出来的，而是从雕刻的门板上发出来的。门板上雕刻的京剧脸谱，宛若皮影戏在门板上飞袖高歌，鼓点敲击着古色古香的门板。京剧，了不起的中国传统艺术啊！

就这样，你从八扇门板上看到了诗词歌赋、陶瓷、书法、相声和历史建筑这八种中国文化的精萃，它们像营养丰富的压缩饼干，浓缩贮存在八个房间。而门板上厚实、庄重、色彩纷呈的鲜活雕纹，正是中国语言既古老又新颖，散发着音韵美的形象诠释。这引起你浓厚的学习兴趣，你决定要走进每一个房间，认真学习中国的语言。

一个甜美的声音在小屋里响起："亲爱的朋友，你学会的不仅是中国语言，还有发挥个人潜力的成功。"

你四处寻找。但是看不见人影儿。她在哪里？她是谁？

"我叫茉莉。我是小屋的主人。我为你服务。我在小屋的每一个空间。"

是的，你看不见她。她的心在小屋的每一个空间。只要你在小屋里，她就与你同在。

我们美丽的茉莉为激励有兴趣学习中国语言的外国学子，用爱心把呕心沥血积累的学习语言的经验筑成奇特的茉莉小屋，流淌着激活兴趣的挚爱。

茉莉喜欢语言，喜欢所有的语言。她知道人类各种语言，都是巴别塔以后，至高者留给人类爱的见证。她从事语言教育多年，掌握多门外语。奇妙的茉莉小屋回响着她温柔甜美的声音，这声音是你心灵里的哪个人？是亲爱的姐妹、是要好的同学、是尊教的师长、是亲如家人的邻舍……这声音给予你的是去效仿至高者最诚挚的爱！去吧——走进每一个房间，去享受你学习的幸福！当你满载中国文化珍品走向远方，可别忘记你也是爱的传递者啊，把茉莉小屋传递给更多的过路人吧！

是为序。

写在前面的话

　　一直以来都想写一本关于如何调动外国人学习中国语言兴趣的书。分享经验也好，阐明自己的见解也好。

　　以我多年学习语言的经验并在某些语种上取得的进步来看，语言的学习不应该是枯燥无味的。相反，语言的学习应该是具有趣味性的。那么，趣味性从何而来呢？首先是从自己所感兴趣的事物上出发。好比我学习了韩语半年左右，便成功取得了韩语 TOPIK 中级证书。除了考前 1 个月集中辅导刷题之外，我走到哪听到哪的韩语歌曲应该居头功。在这本书里，我会介绍我个人认为十分有趣的且具有代表性的中国文化元素与读者们共享，以期调动读者学习汉语言的兴趣。

　　人的趣味是广泛的。在有了知识广度的同时，人们自然会产生对知识深度的需求。因此，在这本书中，我会采用 CAR［构建（Construction）— 应用（Application）—思考（Reflection）］的模式，与读者建立深层对话，旨在让读者成为主动的学习者。另外，考虑到读者的需求，本书采用了中英文对照的形式对内容进行双语阐述。值得一提的是，书中的英文部分并非对中文内容的直接翻译，而是考虑到外国读者的惯性思维和阅读习惯，旨在完整呈现内容的同时兼具逻辑性。

本书的一大特点是图文并举，即每个章节都配有相应的图片，意在引发读者的兴趣且帮助读者进一步加深对内容的理解。本书的另一大特色是非线性文本，即每个章节都相对独立，章节之间并无太多关联。读者可以根据自己的喜好，任意挑选自己中意的章节读起。这也和本书书名——"茉莉之屋"直接呼应。茉莉是我的英文名字，这本书就好似一个大房子，里面有很多房间。每个话题都可以看作一个房间，而每个章节的内容则可以被看作探索不同房间的钥匙。读者——我的访客们可以拿着自己喜欢的钥匙独立地或者结伴而行地来探索某个房间甚至是整个屋子。

恭候各位读者来到茉莉之屋。

Preface

I have thought a lot about writing a book on stimulating foreigners' interest in learning the Chinese language and sharing my experiences and insights.

My journey in learning different languages spans many years. From my perspective, language learning should not be a chore but a pleasure. You may ask, "Where does the joy come from?". I believe that the joy comes from starting with something you are fond of. For example, after learning the Korean language for approximately six months, I successfully obtained the TOPIK (Test of Proficiency in Korean) intermediate-level certificate. In addition to participating in classes, I also listened to my favourite Korean songs throughout the day. This book captures what I personally consider to be very stimulating and representative Chinese cultural elements, and I am pleased to be able to share them with my readers.

In this book, I employ a model called CAR, which is an acronym for construction, application, and reflection. I created this model to connect with my readers and empower them to become active learners. In addition, taking into account readers' needs, this book adopts a bilingual exposition of the content in the form of both Chinese and English sections. It is worth noting that the English sections are not direct translations of the Chinese sections, but are written for foreign readers' mindsets and reading habits, all while presenting the content in full and logically.

A highlight of this book is that each chapter contains relevant images intended to intrigue readers and deepen their understanding of the text. Another prominent feature of this book is its non-linear format; that is, every chapter exists independently. In other words, readers can choose their favourite chapters and read those first. This also echoes the title of the book – *Jasmine's House*. Jasmine is my English name. I envisage the topics in this book as being different rooms, and the content of each chapter as being a room key. So, I hope my readers, or should I say my guests, with different keys in hand, actively and freely explore a room or the entire house either independently or with others.

Finally, welcome to my house.

– Jasmine

茉莉之屋
Jasmine's House

目录
Table of Contents

致 谢

"要常常喜乐，且心存感恩。"

是的。如果没有善于发现喜乐的眼睛，我们会常抱怨世事过于繁杂，生活苦涩难言，亦没有心情去学习新鲜的东西，比如一门新的语言；如果没有感恩的心，我们会觉得凡所得皆理所当然，凡所获皆天经地义，殊不知今日我们取得的些许成就皆来自八方支援。因此在这里，我由衷地向出书过程中给予我帮助的老师及朋友们道一声深深的感谢！

感谢 Helen Sword 老师给予我的早期鼓舞、激励以及文学修辞方面知识的馈赠。如果没有您，这本书可能会推迟几年，甚至极有可能不会问世。

感谢金翠华老师对本书初稿提出的修改建议并应邀写序。您写的书序本身就是一篇美文，且与这本书如此地契合，读起来实在是一种享受。

感谢徐培凡老师对本书终稿中文版的修改指正。能请到您这位资深编辑出山对此书的品质保驾护航，我感到非常的安心。

感谢石芃老师、任锡海老师为本书的封面设计和部分图片拍摄所付出的辛苦和支持。

感谢 Academic Consulting 专业团队对本书终稿英文版的校对。

感谢我的好友 Erika 以及由 Helen Sword 老师所带领的 WriteSPACE 成员们在本书英文诗词翻译上给予的慷慨帮助。

感谢我的好友曦在关于本书图片部分的构思以及收集过程中给予的大力支持。

感谢王媛媛老师在本书出版过程中付出的辛苦和操劳。

最后，感谢我的家人。感谢我的父亲，感谢您时时刻刻对我的帮助和教导。没有您，就没有现在的我。感谢我的先生，谢谢你对我一直是如此的信任和包容。

谨以此书献给我在天堂的妈妈。

Acknowledgements

"Rejoice always and give thanks in all circumstances"

If we lose sight of what brings us joy, we will often complain that the world is too abstruse and that life is full of trivial details. As a result, we may lack the motivation to learn new things, such as a foreign language. If we lack a grateful heart, we will take everything for granted; however, the fact is that all the achievements we have today result from supports we receive from others. Therefore, I would like to express my sincere gratitude to my mentors, friends and family who helped me throughout the process of writing and publishing this book.

Special thanks to my mentor, Dr Helen Sword, for her early inspiration and knowledge of English literary rhetoric. Without her warm encouragement, this book would have been postponed by a few years or perhaps even never eventuated.

I would also like to thank Mrs Jin Cuihua for her insightful feedback on the early draft and for reviewing the book. The review she wrote is beautiful prose in itself, fits so well with this book, and is definitely a pleasure to read. Thanks to Mr Xu Peifan for his thorough amendments to the Chinese version of the final draft. Thanks to Mr Shi Peng and Mr Ren Xihai for their dedication and support for the book cover design and for the photo shoot for this book.

Special thanks to the staff at Academic Consulting, who helped me with the presentation of the English version of the book; to my friend, Erika, and the members of WriteSPACE facilitated by Dr Helen Sword for their generous help in the translation of the poems in the book; to my friend Keny for her valuable advice on photos selected for the book; and to Mrs Wang Yuanyuan for her hard work and dedication in publishing this book.

Finally, I feel incredibly grateful to my father and my husband. Without their support, completing this book would not have been possible.

This book is dedicated to my mom in heaven.

准备读之前

"工欲善其事，必先利其器。"

这句话出自《论语》，意思是工匠想要把工作做好，一定要先使工具锋利，多用来比喻准备工作的重要性。《论语》是一部语录体散文，以记录儒家创始人孔子的言行为主。其中许多内容在当今仍有深远的教育意义。

例如："学而不思则罔，思而不学则殆。"

这句话阐明了学习和思考的辩证关系，意思是如果只学习不思考就会茫然迷惑以至无所得，而只思考不学习则会导致精神疲倦亦无所得。本书所提倡的 CAR 模式［构建（Construction）— 应用（Application）— 思考（Reflection）］则是在学习和思考中间上加入了另一条重要的路径——实践，并系统地把三者串联起来。

想要充分利用好这本书进行语言学习，需要有如下的准备工作：

（1）具备阅读英文或／和中文的能力。

（2）最好基本掌握汉语拼音表以及了解 4 个声调（本书中需要朗读或者背诵的部分会用汉语拼音标注）。

（3）准备一本笔记本和不同颜色的笔（电脑及其他电子用品也可以）。

（4）最好有网络（本书会指导性地给予一些如何在互联网上获取相关资源的信息和方法，以供读者后续的学习、应用和思考）。

来吧，开始你的探索之旅吧。你可以从任何一章读起。

Preparation Before Reading

"Sharp tools make good work/ 工欲善其事，必先利其器 (pronounced: gōng yù shàn qí shì, bì xiān lì qí qì)."

This quotation is from *The Analects of Confucius* and means that if a craftsman wants to do a good job, he must sharpen his tools first. It is often used to metaphorise the importance of preparation. *The Analects of Confucius* mainly contains the words and deeds of Confucius, the founder of Confucianism, much of which still has far-reaching educational significance in Chinese society today. One example of this is "learning without thinking is lost, and thinking without learning is idle/ 学而不思则罔，思而不学则殆 (pronounced: xué ér bù sī zé wǎng, sī ér bù xué zé dài)".

This sentence elucidates the dialectical relationship

between learning and thinking. It means that if one learns without thinking, one may feel dazed and confused and will be harvestless. Conversely, if one thinks without learning, one may feel mentally exhausted and will again be harvestless.

The CAR (Construction – Application – Reflection) model adds another strand – one of "practice", between learning and thinking. As such, this methodology underpins each chapter and attempts to boost the learning process by systematically weaving all three strands together: learning (construction), practice (application), and thinking (reflection).

If you want to make full use of this book for learning the Chinese language, you might want to ensure the following:

1) That you can read in English or Chinese, or both.

2) That you have (ideally) mastered the Chinese Pinyin table and understand the four tones (you will find that some texts that need to be read or recited are marked

with Pinyin in this book).

3) That you have a notebook and pens of different colours on hand (computers and other electronic devices can also be used).

4) That you have internet access, as this book provides some guidance on obtaining relevant internet resources for readers' add-on learning, practicing, and thinking, or CAR – knowledge construction, application, and reflection.

OK, it's time to start your exploration. Please remember you can start with any chapter.

第一章　中国食文化

知识构建 / 应用实践 / 思考感想

知识构建

在马斯洛的需求层次论中，食物被安置在金字塔的底端。食物，是人类赖以生存的基础。食文化，在中国有着历久弥新的意义。

中国的食文化可谓当今世界之最！它历史悠久、品种繁多。无论在选材、制作工艺还是饮食风俗上，根据地域的不同皆有差异。经过千年的演变，发展成广为人知的四个大的菜系：鲁菜、川菜、粤菜和苏菜。鲁是山东的简称，所以鲁菜即山东菜。鲁菜品种多样，味道偏于鲜咸。代表菜有葱烧海参、红烧大虾等。川是四川的简称，川菜讲究的是麻辣。代表菜有麻婆豆腐、夫妻肺片等。看到这里，不知你心中是否有这样的疑问：豆腐和麻婆有什么关系？夫妻肺片应该不是字面上看到的如此恐怖的意思吧？ 在介绍苏菜和粤菜之前，我先来讲讲这两道菜背后的故事。相传麻婆豆腐是由清代成都一位面部有麻子的女人所创，味道堪称一绝。不仅麻辣鲜咸兼具，而且豆腐入口软嫩细滑。麻婆豆腐由此得名。而夫妻肺片则是根据 20 世纪 30 年代成都一对专卖凉拌牛杂的夫妇所命名的。牛杂因包含牛心、牛舌、牛肚等，所以早先被称为"废片"。后来因为"废"字不好听，选了同音字"肺"来替代。

　　苏菜，也被称为淮扬菜。和鲁菜、川菜味道的大开大合不同，苏菜讲究精致，味道也偏温和。代表菜有清炖狮子头、松鼠鳜鱼[1]等。有了前面的故事铺垫，你们脑海中是不是应该有了对菜名的理解？清炖狮子头应该和狮子没关系，松鼠鳜鱼也没有松鼠什么事。没错，这两道菜是根据其形状而命名。狮子头实际是肥瘦相间的肉丸子。肉丸经煮熟后，肥肉瘦肉分离，显得玲珑有致。因形状酷似雄狮头，故在唐代时期被某官员赋予狮子头的美名。清炖狮子头秉承淮扬菜的特点：味道鲜香，肥而不腻。松鼠鳜鱼的名字来头更大。相传乾隆皇帝到苏州，

1　见 17 页图。

当地厨师为讨其欢心而别出心裁，把鱼烧成扬尾的松鼠形状。乾隆帝吃罢大加赞赏，松鼠鳜鱼由此得名。

粤菜即广东菜。粤菜偏清淡，追求食物本身的味道呈现。粤菜的代表菜为白切鸡、白灼虾等。我个人对粤菜比较感兴趣的部分是它丰富多样的早茶小吃。和大家分享一下我吃过的广式早茶[1]中中意的美食吧。

香港及内地南方部分地区讲的是广东话 / 粤语。它和普通话很大的区别在于有九声六调，并且拼音表也不相同。粤语拼音，简称粤拼，是香港语言学学会在 1993 年制定的罗马化拼音方案，这对于想要系统学习广东话的外国学习者是一个福音。值得一提的是，自香港 1997 年回归祖国，普通话也在该地区普及了起来。再加上香港融合的多语环境，就算不会说粤语，也一样可以在香港生活、工作和学习。在这里附上一个我个人认为非常不错的油管频道：Learn Cantonese with CantoneseClass101。如果对学习粤语有兴趣的朋友，可以自行研究。

1　见 18 页图。

应用实践

"想要知道梨子的滋味，就要亲口尝一尝。"想要掌握一门语言，就要亲自用一用。在自己生活的城市或地区找一家广式餐厅，约上朋友家人一起去吃早茶，尝试用学到的词点餐吧。（即使餐牌看不懂也没关系。）

现如今网络资源丰富，许多以前难求的菜谱，现在动动手指都能在网络上找到。我有一位新西兰朋友酷爱中国美食，根据网上找到的菜谱，已经成功地在家里烹饪出许多他喜欢的菜肴。如果正在读此书的你也是一名"吃货"，不妨上网找找感兴趣的菜谱，自己动手试试看吧。（友情提示：调料在华人超市都有售哦！）

思考感想

想一想，你对中国的什么地区感兴趣？可以自己上网查查那里的美食。比如"川菜"。想要知道读法，可以把吸引你的美食的英文名称键入搜索引擎。比如"Dan Dan Noodles"[1]。除相关的介绍之外，绝大多数情况下你会很幸运地看到相关的汉字："担担面"。然后将汉字复制粘贴到搜索引擎。搜索时别忘记加上"Pinyin"[2]。这样，你就可以找到它的读音"dàn dàn miàn"了。你是不是惊喜地发现中文的拼音"dàn dàn miàn"和你之前看到的英文翻译"Dan Dan Noodles"好像差不多。没错，不少饮食上的翻译还是保证了原语言的原汁原味。这样一来，说不定你在不知不觉中已经掌握很多中文的单词和发音了。

　　再想想，你在附近的中餐外卖店有没有点过"chow mein"？这其实是为了外国人发音方便，按照英文发音规则演变而来的。正宗的中文发音是"chǎo miàn"。善于总结的你会发现"miàn"就是"noodles"。所以尝试举一反三，想想你还喜欢吃什么"miàn"吧。哦，对了，如果在中餐店遇到年纪相对比较大的华人，说"chǎo miàn"他／她有可能听不懂哦。这个时候用粤拼"caau2 min6"试试看吧，说不定有意外的惊喜哦！

1　见 19 页截屏。
2　见 19 页截屏。

松鼠鳜鱼

Deep-fried Mandarin Fish

广式早茶

Dim Sum

Dan Dan Noodles   ✕   🎤   🔍

https://www.recipetineats.com › Noodles

Dan Dan Noodles (Spicy Sichuan noodles) | RecipeTin Eats

2020年2月3日 — Dan Dan Noodles – the iconic spicy Sichuan noodles, a flavour explosion with slippery noodles tossed in an intense sesame chilli sauce and ...

https://omnivorescookbook.com › dan-dan-no...

Dan Dan Noodles (担担面) - Omnivore's Cookbook

Dan Dan Noodles (担担面, dan dan mian) are one of the most famous of Sichuan street foods. The freshly boiled thin noodles are served in a savory, spicy sauce ...

https://www.halfbakedharvest.com › better-tha...

Better Than Takeout Dan Dan Noodles. - Half Baked Harvest

2019年10月22日 — If you're not familiar with Dan Dan noodles, they are spicy Chinese noodles with a dark sauce that usually contains preserved vegetables, chili ...

https://redhousespice.com › dan-dan-noodles

Dan Dan Noodles (Spicy Sichuan Noodles, 担担面) - Red ...

2020年2月12日 — Dan Dan noodles (担担面, aka spicy Sichuan noodles) is named after the traditional carrying pole "Dan Dan" that street vendors use.

担担面 Pinyin   ✕   🎤

http://www.zwbit.com › translate › 担担面 ▾

担担面 - ZWBit 汉字

Pinyin Simplified Chinese, English, Traditional Chinese. dàndànmiàn · 担担面, Sichuan noodles with a spicy and numbing sauce;, 擔擔面 ...

截屏

Screenshots

Chapter 1: Chinese Food Culture/ 中国食文化

(pronounced: zhōngguó shí wénhuà)

Construction

In Maslow's hierarchy of needs, physiological needs (which are basic or survival needs), including air, water, and food, are placed at the bottom of the pyramid. Food is a fundamental requirement for human beings to live. However, food culture in China has further significance.

Across the world, China's food culture is extraordinary and reputed for its long history and a wide variety of cuisines. There is tremendous diversity among different regions of China in terms of ingredient selection, cooking techniques, and local dietary habits.

From thousands of years of evolution, four great traditions of Chinese cuisine have been developed. These great traditions are Lu cuisine, Chuan cuisine, Yue cuisine, and Su cuisine.

Lu is another name for Shandong province. Lu cuisine/ 鲁菜 (pronounced: lǔ cài) contains a wide range of varieties of dishes, and these dishes primarily taste fresh and salty. Representative dishes include braised sea cucumber with scallion/ 葱烧海参 (pronounced: cōng shāo hǎi shēn) and braised prawns/ 红烧大虾 (pronounced: hóng shāo dà xiā). Chuan is another name for Sichuan province. Chuan cuisine/ 川菜 (pronounced: chuān cài) features numbing-hotness and spiciness. Mapo tofu/ 麻婆豆腐 (pronounced: má pó dòu fu) and beef lungs in chilli sauce/ 夫妻肺片 (pronounced: fū qī fèi piàn) are examples of dishes from Sichuan province.

When seeking the English translation of these dish names, I found that some translations did not always fully address the dishes' cultural and historical contexts.

Translations sometimes neglect to include the inspiring and compelling stories behind the original Chinese names. For example, mapo/ 麻婆 in the Chinese language means a pockmarked woman. The story originates from the Qing Dynasty. In Chengdu, a city in Sichuan province, a lady with pockmarks on her face created a special tofu dish. The dish was unique in that it was numbingly hot and spicy, but also soft, tender, and melted in the mouth. Therefore, the dish was named after Mapo, the creator of the yummy dish.

The original name of a dish mentioned earlier, beef lungs in chilli sauce, may sound a bit gruesome if translated literally. The literal translation of this dish is couple (husband and wife) lungs. As a matter of fact, the dish was named after a couple who sold cold mixed beef offal in Chengdu in the 1930s. Beef offal, including beef lungs, hearts, tongues, and tripe was previously called waste pieces/ 废片 (pronounced: fèi piàn). However, people did not like the name because the word "waste/

废 (pronounced: fèi)" did not sound appropriate for food. Therefore, they considered a homonym " 肺 / lung (pronounced: fèi)" to replace the word "waste/ 废 (pronounced: fèi)". Now that you know the story behind this dish, you may be surprised to know that beef lungs in chilli sauce contain not only beef lungs, but hearts, tongues, and tripe. This is an example of an English translation failing to reveal a Chinese dish's real and true substance.

Su cuisine/ 苏菜 (pronounced: sū cài) is sometimes referred to as Huaiyang cuisine/ 淮扬菜 (pronounced: huái yáng cài). Unlike Lu and Chuan dishes, Su dishes are exquisitely presented and taste light and mild. Stewed pork ball/ 清炖狮子头 (pronounced: qīng dùn shī zi tóu) and deep-fried mandarin fish[1]/ 松鼠鳜鱼 (pronounced: sōng shǔ guì yú) are two examples of delicacies from Su. However, the English translations of these dish names

---

1   See picture on page 17.

lack essence because they omit an interesting component – the appearance of the dishes. The original Chinese names of stewed "lion-head-shaped" pork ball and deep-fried "squirrel-shaped" mandarin fish, focus on the dishes' appealing presentations.

An official of the Tang Dynasty coined the imaginative name stewed lion-head-shaped pork ball after prudently observing the dish's appearance. Once the meatball was well cooked, the mixture of fat and lean would be separated, bearing a great resemblance to a lion's head. Stewed pork ball embodies the characteristics of Huaiyang cuisine as it tastes fresh and is not greasy. The origin of the name for deep-fried squirrel-shaped mandarin fish is even more interesting. It is said that during the Qing Dynasty, the Qianlong Emperor visited Suzhou, a city in Jiangsu province. To please the emperor, the local chef ingeniously fried the fish into the shape of a squirrel with a raised tail. The Qianlong Emperor was highly impressed with the dish, and this vivid depiction of the dish became esteemed and worshipped.

Yue cuisine/ 粤菜 (pronounced: yuè cài) refers to Guangdong or Cantonese cuisine, which is always light and preserves the authentic taste of the ingredients. Examples of representative dishes are plain boiled chicken/ 白切鸡 (pronounced: bái qiē jī) and scalded prawns/ 白灼虾 (pronounced: bái zhuó xiā). I am personally fond of Cantonese traditional brunch, which is also known as yum cha/ 饮茶 (pronounced: yǐn chá). Yum cha includes rich and diverse dim sum/ 点心 (pronounced: diǎn xīn) and Chinese tea. Here I would like to share a couple of pictures of what I had for dim sum meals[1] at some Cantonese restaurants.

Noticeably, Cantonese/ 粤语 (pronounced: yuè yǔ) is spoken in Hong Kong and some regions of southern mainland China. Unlike Mandarin, Cantonese has six tones, and the Pinyin table is also different. Cantonese

1   See picture on page 18.

Pinyin, also called Jyutping/ 粤拼 (pronounced: yuè pīn), was formulated by the Linguistic Society of Hong Kong in 1993. This romanised Pinyin scheme serves well for foreign learners who decide to learn Cantonese systematically. Since Hong Kong's return to China in 1997, it is worth noting that Mandarin has also been widely spoken in that region. The multilingual environment guarantees that those who cannot speak Cantonese can live, work and study in Hong Kong.

I would like to recommend a YouTube channel that I personally find very useful: Learn Cantonese with CantoneseClass101. If you are ever interested in learning Cantonese, you can explore it yourself.

Application

In China, there is a saying that "If you want to know

the taste of pears, you have to taste them yourself". Similarly, if you want to master a language, you need to use it. So please find a Cantonese restaurant in your city or area and invite your friends and family to have some dim sum while enjoying Chinese tea. Try to order the food by using the vocabulary and/or sentences you have learned (it does not matter if you cannot understand the Chinese-written menu).

Nowadays, you can find many resources on Chinese food on the internet. Many recipes that were hard to find in the past can now be found by simply clicking a mouse with your finger. I have a New Zealand friend who loves Chinese food and has successfully cooked many dishes he likes based on recipes he found online. If you are a foodie, you might want to look for recipes on the internet that you are fascinated about and try to cook them yourself. A friendly tip – seasonings are always available in Chinese supermarkets!

Reflection

What part/region of China are you curious about?
You can search for local food, such as Chuan cuisine/
川菜 online. If you want to learn the pronunciation of
certain Chinese dishes, you can type the English words
(such as "Dan Dan Noodles") in the search box[1]. You will
find the relevant information and will most likely to see
the corresponding Chinese characters written as " 担担
面 ". Then, you can copy and paste the Chinese characters
into the search box. Do not forget to add "Pinyin/ 拼音 "
this time[2]. Consequently, you will see the pronunciation
"dàn dàn miàn" appear.

Are you surprised that the Chinese Pinyin dàn dàn
miàn looks very similar to the English translation Dan
Dan Noodles? You will find that some translations retain

---

1   See screenshot on page 19.
2   See screenshot on page 19.

the authentic part of the original language. By the same token, you may have already mastered some Chinese words or pronunciations without even noticing.

Have you ever ordered chow mein at a local Chinese takeaway? The Chinese Mandarin pronunciation is chǎo miàn. And yes, "noodles" in Chinese is pronounced as "miàn". So, try to draw some inferences from your knowledge pool and think about what kind of "miàn" you like most.

By the way, if an elderly Chinese person takes your order at your local takeaway, they may not understand your Mandarin pronunciation of chǎo miàn. In this case, you might try Jyutping "caau2 min6". Good luck on your new adventure!

茉莉之屋
Jasmine's House

第二章　中国茶文化

知识构建 / 应用实践 / 思考感想

知识构建

　　说到饮茶，是不是首先想到的是我们第一章所讲的广式早茶？广式早茶之所以被叫作"饮茶"，实际是从粤语"叹茶"而来，有享受一盅茶之意。与其说重在吃或者喝茶，不如说享受生活的小确幸。（注：小确幸是一个缩略语，指的是小小的确定的幸福，源于日本作家村上春树的文集《兰格汉斯岛的午后》。）

　　这一章所讲的中国茶文化涉及不同方面。据说中国人发现茶是在神农时代，但是形成一种茶道文化则是在唐代。唐代曾有过万邦来朝的开元盛世，其经济文化都有过飞速的发展。唐代中期，陆羽撰写的《茶经》是世界上最早有关茶的文献，他也因此被誉为茶圣。

中国茶分六大种类，除大家熟知的红茶、绿茶外，还有乌龙茶、黄茶、白茶和黑茶。下面列出一些我平时在闲暇时特别喜欢品的茶，也顺便科普一下不同茶的冲泡[1]小知识。

种类	名称	冲泡的适宜水温	冲泡的适宜器皿
绿茶	西湖龙井	80~85℃	透明玻璃杯
红茶	祁门红茶	95℃以上	紫砂茶具
乌龙茶	凤凰单丛	100℃	浅色瓷茶具[2]
黑茶	普洱茶	90℃	紫砂茶具

黄茶和白茶我平时喝得很少，了解得也不多，在这里不便推荐。建议大家在冲泡不同茶叶的时候把控好温度。因为温度过高或过低都会影响茶的口感以及破坏它的营养成分。如果大家的中文阅读能力较好，推荐詹詹老师编著的《一席茶》。书中有很多关于茶席设计和茶道美学的见解，我读后觉得十分受用。

---

1 见 37 页图。
2 见 38 页图。

应用实践

找一间风雅的茶室或咖啡馆吧，点上一杯茶，打开随身携带的笔记本，随便写写当下的心情吧。

或者在家里冲泡一杯自己喜欢的茶，打开手机或者电脑的搜索引擎继续来探索中国的茶文化是如何传到西方国家的吧。建议搜索关键词："丝绸之路""茶马古道"。

思考感想

和我名字相关的一种茶叫茉莉花茶，在中国北方地区非常受欢迎。它的香气迷人，但是严格算起来却不属于中国的六大茶系。想知道为什么吗？利用网络搜索看看吧。

另外，现如今茶文化在许多国家极度盛行。不过我偶尔也会思考关于其形式和内涵之间的辩证关系。在这里推荐给大家一篇延展阅读——《也说"茶"》。这是我父亲写的一篇散文，收录在他的《虎城文影》一书中。我把整篇文章翻译成英文，供大家阅读参考。

也说"茶"

古往今来，有关茶的讲究颇多。大多围绕着茶类、茶艺、茶礼（礼仪）、茶境（场所）、茶道等五个方面而论。初论者倒也平实，论及的大体是茶类、茶艺等物质层面的东西。后论者逐渐"高深"，直到把喝茶推到宗教高度上，实不足取。

喝茶对人体的益处自不必说，喝茶的确还能令人生发出异样的感觉来。因为茶如同饮酒一样，三巡过后，飘飘欲仙，吆三喝四，个个争抢话语权。然而茶要比酒雅，过去所谓的"文人雅趣"，指的就是琴棋书画酒诗茶。自古以来茶香与书香、墨香齐名（号称"三香"），是高雅、淡定精神之体现。正所谓"文人不可一日无茶"。在中国，茶也不只是文人雅士的独有品。平头百姓、草履布衣一样好茶，俗称"柴米油盐酱醋茶"。可见，茶也是人们生活中的必需品。文人墨客，一茗在手，谈古论今；芸芸众生，茶水一碗，照样海阔天空。如果过分强调茶境、茶礼，甚至说喝茶能喝到睁开第三只眼睛，那纯属故弄玄虚，缘于犯了垄断癖！茶境再优雅，茶礼再讲究，若多人一起喝，断喝不出什么韵致来，充其量是润喉解渴而已。

人生如旅，奔波劳碌之人停下脚步，小憩片刻，一壶香茗，享受些许闲适。这本身就是放下。要说这个放下与禅意的"放下"吻合在一起，所谓"禅茶一味"也不是不可。但这是喝茶升发出的韵致，属茶道范畴。它跟宗教完全是两码事。

宁静淡泊茶之品，感悟人生茶之道。是也！

冲泡
Brewing

茶具

Tea Utensil Sets

Chapter 2: Chinese Tea Culture/中国茶文化

(pronounced: zhōngguó chá wénhuà)

Construction

When it comes to tea/ 茶 (pronounced: chá), do you initially think of yum cha mentioned in Chapter 1? Although yum cha literally means drinking tea, it actually implies enjoying tea with dim sum, which is adapted from the Cantonese words 叹茶 . " 叹 " in Cantonese means to enjoy. Thus, instead of merely focusing on food and drink, yum cha represents an attitude to life – enjoying small but certain happiness /" 小确幸 "– in other words, living in the present.

P.S. 小确幸 (pronounced: xiǎo què xìng) means "small

but certain happiness" in Chinese and has become a catchphrase among young people in China. This expression was originally drawn from the book *Afternoon in the Islets of Langerhans*, written by a Japanese writer, Haruki Murakami.

This chapter recounts various aspects of Chinese tea culture. It is believed that tea was first discovered in China in the Shen Nong era and that tea culture was gradually formed and developed in the Tang Dynasty. Noticeably, during the Kaiyuan reign, the Tang Empire experienced unprecedented economic, cultural, and political development. In the middle Tang era, Lu Yu wrote a book called *The Classic of Tea* / 茶经 (pronounced: chá jīng), which is the earliest mention of tea in the world. Lu Yu is therefore respected as the sage of tea for his enormous contributions.

Chinese tea can be subsumed under six broad categories. Besides the well-known black tea and green tea, there is also oolong tea, yellow tea, white tea, and dark tea. I have listed some kinds of tea in the following table that I like to sip. Following the table are some tips that I would like to share regarding the brewing[1] of different teas.

Categories	Name	Proper tea brewing temperature	Proper utensils
Green tea/ 绿茶 (pronounced: lǜ chá)	Longjing tea/ 龙井茶 (pronounced: lóng-jǐng chá)	80°C–85°C	Transparent glasses
Black tea/ 红茶 (pronounced: hóng chá)	Keemun Black tea/ 祁门红茶 (pronounced: qímén hóng chá)	95°C above	Yixing clay teapots and teacups
Oolong tea/ 乌龙茶 (pronounced: wū lóng chá)	Phoenix dan cong/ 凤凰单丛 (pronounced: fèng-huáng dān cóng)	100°C	Light coloured porcelain teapots and teacups[2]
Dark tea/ 黑茶 (pronounced: hēi chá)	Pu-erh/ 普洱茶 (pronounced: pǔěr chá)	90°C	Yixing clay teapots and teacups

---

1   See picture on page 37.
2   See picture on page 38.

I barely drink yellow tea or white tea and lack first-hand information about them. Thus, it is not appropriate for me to comment on these. Notably, the brewing temperature is very crucial when making tea. The taste and nutrients might be affected to a certain degree if the brewing temperature is too high or low. I highly recommend the book *Yi Xi Cha/ 一席茶* by Zhan Zhan, which contains a significant amount of information and knowledge regarding tea table settings, customs, and etiquette in Chinese tea drinking and tea ceremonies, which I find very practical and stimulating.

Application

Please find an elegant tea house or café where you can have a cup of tea. Then, grab a notebook and a pen, and try to write down how you feel about the tea you ordered and the aesthetics of the surroundings.

You could also make a cup of tea by yourself at home while using the internet to dive into how Chinese tea culture has spread to Western countries. In the search box, you can type keywords, such as "Silk Road/ 丝绸之路 (pronounced: sī chóu zhī lù)" and "Tea Horse Road/ 茶马古道 (pronounced: chá mǎ gǔ dào)".

Reflection

A tea that is related to my name is Jasmine tea, which tea drinkers in northern China admire. Its aroma is very charming. But guess what? Strictly speaking, it does not belong to China's six tea families. Do you want to know why? Please use the internet to discover the answer by yourself.

Nowadays, tea culture is popular in many countries. However, I often wonder about the superficial appreciation of tea versus the real understanding of tea.

Here I will recommend some supplementary reading material – *A Talk About "Tea"*. This is prose extracted from the book *Hu Cheng Wen Ying / 虎城文影* written by my father, Wang Hucheng. I have translated the article and hope it will show you some different perspectives regarding how tea culture can be perceived and interpreted.

A Talk About "Tea"

Until now, there have been many theories and assumptions about tea. Tea categories, customs and etiquette when drinking tea, the environment for drinking tea (place), and tea ceremonies are often popular discussion topics among tea lovers. It is usually common to start talking about types of tea and ceremonies, which is superficial but also practical. However, some discussions regarding tea are becoming "unfathomable", with some people correlating tea culture to religion, which seems ridiculous.

One of the many benefits of drinking tea is that it can make people feel pleased. Tea contains caffeine, so like drinking alcohol, people may feel relaxed and start to talk with eloquence after having cups of tea. However, tea is considered more elegant than wine. In the past, the so-called "literati elegance/ 文人雅趣 (pronounced: wén rén yǎ qù)" appreciated music, chess, calligraphy, painting, wine, poetry, and tea. From ancient times to the present, the aroma of tea is on par with the aroma of books and ink (known together as the "Three Aromas"), all of which can be seen as the embodiment of gracefulness and calm. There is also a saying that the "Literati cannot live without tea".

However, tea is not only for literati and scholars. Ordinary people also enjoy tea. A common phrase used to describe people's life necessities is "firewood, rice, oil, salt, soy sauce, vinegar and tea", which highlights the importance of tea. Literati, with a cup of posh tea, perhaps like to comment on current affairs; folks, with a bowl of not-so-posh tea, perhaps like to discuss everyday life anecdotes. If some people overemphasise tea rituals or the environment for drinking tea, or even say that drinking tea can help open the third eye, it will be purely ironic! It does not matter how aesthetic the environment is and how exquisite the tea ceremony is; if people swarm to guzzle tea together, they will be unable to tell how good the tea is. At best, all they can do is moisten their throat and quench their thirst.

Life is like a journey. People living in the hustle and bustle could stop, take a break, have a cup of tea, and enjoy the moment. This is to let go, which is similar to the Zen concept of "drop". This can also be understood as a form of mediation, which by no means should be confused with religion.

Tea can help people find tranquillity, thus leading to rational contemplation!

第三章 中国陶瓷

知识构建 / 应用实践 / 思考感想

知识构建

　　善于总结的朋友应该已经发现关于茶具挑选的规律：茶汤颜色越浅的越应该使用透明玻璃杯或者浅色瓷茶具；反之，茶汤颜色越深的越应该使用颜色比较厚重的茶具，比如说紫砂壶[1]。

　　紫砂壶相传源于宋代，后在明代盛行。紫砂壶以江苏宜兴出产的为上品。长期使用紫砂壶，壶内会形成"茶山"，即厚厚的一层茶垢。因此，不用放茶叶，只放清水便有茶香。紫砂壶因其盛名身价不菲。据说大师级的茶壶作品价值人民币 7 位数。

1　见 52 页图。

中国的烧陶术可以再往上追溯数千年到新石器时代。我想到我的父亲几年前曾参与过一部以广西钦州龙窑为背景的电影拍摄。龙窑本质上就是烧制陶器的柴窑。其拱起的窑膛自下而上近百米，形状酷似一条卧龙，因而得名。钦州坭兴陶泥料取自钦江两岸红白两色土，混成后入窑时呈米黄色，出窑后经过打磨显现五色暗彩。堪称一绝！正因如此，广西钦州龙窑烧制的坭兴陶器排在中国四大名陶第二位。在此附上我父亲当年参观龙窑之后即兴所做的诗一首。

龙窑礼献

王虎城

火生六百载，焰接尧舜朝。

进炉清一色，出窑彩虹飘。

四海漂流客，聚桂绘兴陶。

弘扬祖宗业，力微也荣耀。

制陶非中国独有，然而中国在制陶的基础上进一步研究实践，发明了瓷器。像在明代成为瓷器主流品种之一的"青花瓷"世界闻名。说到瓷器，就不得不讲到出产瓷器的圣地——景德镇市。中国有句老话叫"一方水土养一方人"，用在这里也是恰当的。景德镇之所以脱颖而出，跟它的"水土"有很大关系。具体来说，景德镇一带的"土"是制造好瓷的先决条件；景德镇四通八达的"水路"方便了瓷器的运输，为后续的贸易提供了便利。景德镇瓷器曾一度被英国贵族所推崇，其价格也水涨船高。

多年前我去北京和苏州旅行时，有幸在当地博物馆观看了几件国宝级陶瓷品。先人的智慧令我大为惊讶！我切身感受到了那些文物所承载的历史与文化的厚重感。如果有机会，我建议大家一定要去亲身体验一下。

应用实践

用"博物馆里有什么？"这个游戏考验一下自己的中文单词量和记忆力吧！

A：博物馆里有什么？

B：博物馆里有陶器。（转向下一人提问）博物馆里有什么?

C:博物馆里有陶器,有瓷器。(转向下一人提问)博物馆里有什么?

D:博物馆里有陶器,有瓷器,有……

继续……

思考感想

收藏一两件陶器[1]、瓷器[2]摆放在家里,你会觉得室内雅气顿增。用眼睛去观察,领略其视觉之美;用手去触碰,享受其质感之丰盈;用心去感知,这样的静态物体给你带来怎样的精神层面的感受:愉悦?平静?抑或其他?

1 见 53 页图。
2 见 54 页图。

紫砂茶具
Yixing Teaware

彩陶

Painted Pottery

青花瓷瓶

Blue and White Porcelain Vase

Chapter 3: Chinese Ceramics/ 中国陶瓷

(pronounced: zhōngguó táocí)

Construction

From the tips I gave you in the previous chapter, you may now have a general idea about choosing proper tea sets. For example, for lighter coloured teas, transparent glass or lighter coloured porcelain utensils should be used. In contrast, for a darker coloured tea, a deeper coloured tea set should be considered, such as Yixing teaware[1].

It is believed that Yixing ware originated during

---

1   See picture on page 52.

the Song Dynasty and has gained fame since the Ming Dynasty. Yixing is a city located in Jiangsu province and is thought of as the original location of the particular clay. The uniqueness of the Yixing clay teapot is its endearingly durable cha shan/ 茶山 (pronounced: chá shān), which is a thick layer of tea stains formed inside the pot over time. With a layer of tea stains, the aroma of tea will emerge from only pouring hot water into the teapot. As a result, Yixing clay teaware has become very prized, and allegedly, a masterclass teapot can be valued at seven figures.

The history of Chinese pottery can be traced back thousands of years to the Neolithic age. My father took part in a movie production years ago, set in the contextual backdrop of pottery-making in the Dragon kiln workshop in Qinzhou city, Guangxi. The kiln is fuelled by wood for firing, burning, and drying wares. Its arched hearth is nearly 100 metres long, paralleling a lying dragon. The clay is gathered from the red and white soil on the banks of Qinjiang river nearby. After mixing, the colour of the clay turns beige. Once coming out of the kiln after being heated and fired, the pottery is crafted using grinding wheels. Then, guess what? It will become colourful even without glazing. Absolutely amazing, right? Because of its distinctiveness, Nixing pottery, the pottery fired in the Dragon kiln ranks second among China's four renowned categories of potteries.

Below is a poem that my father wrote after he visited the Dragon kiln, which I hope can help you sense the beauty of pottery-making without going to the Dragon kiln site in person.

龙窑礼献

lóngyáo lǐxiàn

王虎城

Wang Hucheng

火生六百载，焰接尧舜朝。

huǒ shēng liù bǎi zǎi, yàn jiē yáo shùn cháo.

进炉清一色，出窑彩虹飘。

jìn lú qīng yī sè, chū yáo cǎihóng piāo.

四海漂流客，聚桂绘兴陶。

sìhǎi piāoliú kè, jù guì huì xīng táo.

弘扬祖宗业，力微也荣耀。

hóngyáng zǔzōng yè, lì wēi yě róngyào.

Dragon Kiln

Six-hundred-year-old fire, flame of Yao and Shun
We see the holy grail of generations.

Beige turns to colour
Fire burns in the kiln.

Drifters flock to Guangxi
To craft beautiful things, tangible and intangible.

Treading the ancestral path
Unearthing the wisdom of those who came before us
Honouring the gifts of those yet to come.

Low-fired ceramics are not identified with China. Nonetheless, Chinese people have further studied and practised pottery craft and eventually invented porcelain – china. Among the mainstream varieties, blue and white porcelain is famous around the world. Jingdezhen, a city in Jiangxi province, is regarded as the origin of porcelain products in China. An old Chinese saying is that "the unique features of a local environment always endue special characteristics to its inhabitants", which also explains why Jingdezhen porcelain stands out. The soil in Jingdezhen is a prerequisite for producing quality porcelain; the integrated waterway throughout Jingdezhen facilitates the smooth transportation of porcelain products and paves the way for further trading. Jingdezhen porcelain once enjoyed quite a reputation among British aristocrats, and the price was also once unaffordable to ordinary folks.

A couple of years ago, I travelled to Beijing and Suzhou and admired several original first-class ceramics exhibited in local museums. However, I found it difficult to unwind my complex tangled ideas at the time. Besides the visual stimuli, I could also sense something intangible, similar to a feeling of sombreness. Therefore, if you have got time, I strongly recommend you go there and embark on a journey of discovery by yourself.

Application

I would like to introduce a game called "What can you find in a museum?". You can play the game with your friends to test your Chinese vocabulary (and memory).

A: "What can you find in a museum?"

B: "Pottery/ 陶器 (pronounced: táo qì). (Head to the next person) What can you find in a museum?"

C: "Pottery/ 陶器 (pronounced: táo qì) and porcelain/ 瓷器 (pronounced: cí qì). (Head to the next person) What can you find in a museum?"

D: "Pottery/ 陶器 (pronounced: táo qì), porcelain/ 瓷器 (pronounced: cí qì), and…."

Continue…

Reflection

Please try to collect one or two pieces of pottery[1] or porcelain[2] and place them in your home. Observe them and appreciate the visual beauty. Touch them with your

---

1　See picture on page 53.
2　See picture on page 54.

fingers and feel the tactile textures. Become aware with your heart — what kind of spiritual comfort do such static objects bring to you — pleasure, calm, or something else?

第四章　中国诗词

知识构建 / 应用实践 / 思考感想

知识构建

中国的古诗词是中华民族文化的一种文学形式。是地道的
土特产。

中国"诗"的产生可以追溯到西周时期。汉代乐府文化盛
行，乐府诗为了配合乐器演唱，慢慢演化成"词"。诗在唐代
盛行，词在宋代达到顶峰。这也是为什么如今我们谈起中国诗
词，会有"唐诗宋词"的说法。

诗词讲究格律、平仄、押韵等。在这章我想重点聊一聊平
仄押韵的问题。古汉语中有"平上去入"四声，而现代标准汉
语中只有"平上去"三声。说到这里，可能有朋友有疑问："我
们在学汉语拼音时学到的明明是四声啊？"汉语拼音中的四声

实际是"平上去"中的"平"声分出"阴平"和"阳平"再加上"上"和"去"——即"一声"（Tāng/ 汤）、"二声"（Táng/ 糖）、"三声"（Tǎng/ 躺）和"四声"（Tàng/ 烫）。

值得注意的是，"入"声目前在普通话中已经没有了，但是在中国部分地区的方言中仍然存在。因为很多古代的名诗人、词人的籍贯都是南方，所以他们会在诗词中大量使用"去"声字。这就解释了为什么很多汉语学习者在用普通话读诗词时，发现有些词句并不符合平仄的原则，不押韵。

下面和大家分享两首我非常喜欢的诗和词。

将进酒

李白

君不见，黄河之水天上来，奔流到海不复回。

君不见，高堂明镜悲白发，朝如青丝暮成雪。

人生得意须尽欢，莫使金樽空对月。

天生我材必有用，千金散尽还复来。

烹羊宰牛且为乐，会须一饮三百杯。

岑夫子，丹丘生，将进酒，杯莫停。

与君歌一曲，请君为我倾耳听。

钟鼓馔玉不足贵，但愿长醉不复醒。

古来圣贤皆寂寞，惟有饮者留其名。

陈王昔时宴平乐，斗酒十千恣欢谑。

主人何为言少钱，径须沽取对君酌。

五花马，千金裘，

呼儿将出换美酒，与尔同销万古愁。

李白，字太白，号青莲居士，唐代杰出的浪漫主义诗人。其诗传世甚广，其中不少名篇成千古绝唱。李白善诗且豪饮，有"诗仙""酒圣"之称。

一剪梅

李清照

红藕香残玉簟秋，轻解罗裳，独上兰舟。

云中谁寄锦书来？雁字回时，月满西楼。

花自飘零水自流，一种相思，两处闲愁。

此情无计可消除，才下眉头，却上心头。

李清照，号易安居士，宋代著名女词人，婉约派代表。李清照一生命运多舛，前半生与丈夫赵明诚度过一段岁月静好时光，后半生因国破家亡在颠沛流离中苟生。

应用实践

利用网络查看一下我推荐的两首诗词的翻译吧。看看和自己理解的是否差不多。另外，如果有对诗词感兴趣的朋友，我给大家推荐一个特别好用的应用程序——"学堂在线"。这里收录了中国各大名校的精品课，而且很多课程都是免费的哦。值得一提的是，我曾利用闲暇时间学习了清华大学王步高教授主讲的"唐宋词鉴赏"，受益匪浅。我也曾想过以写信的形式向王教授表达感谢之情，无奈得知先生已仙逝。遗憾！在此借由本书的发表，向未曾谋面的老师表达最深的敬意！

思考感想

  诗人词人通常以一种凝练的方式或言志或抒情。大家可以想一想在自己的国家，有没有你特别喜欢或欣赏的诗人？有没有可以信手拈来的诗？有的话，在笔记本上记录下来吧。

  如果你对中国诗词有一定的研究的话，也请想一想中西方诗人在语言和情感的表达上有什么不同吧。

Chapter 4: Chinese Poetry/ 中国诗词

(pronounced: zhōngguó shī cí)

Construction

Chinese poetry, including shi/ 诗 (pronounced: shī) and ci/ 词 (pronounced: cí), is the literary form unique to Chinese culture. It can therefore be viewed as a veritable Chinese local product.

The origin of the Chinese word "shi" can be traced back to the Western Zhou Dynasty. In the Han Dynasty, a Chinese governmental department called Yuefu/ 乐 府 (pronounced: yuè fǔ), also known as the Imperial Music Bureau, was mainly charged with tasks related to music, poems, religious rituals, and entertainment. Unlike other forms of poetry, Yuefu poems were composed to be sung along with musical instruments, thus gradually evolving into "ci". Shi flourished in the Tang Dynasty, while ci prospered in the Song Dynasty. That is why when it comes to Chinese poetry, there is a saying of "tang shi/ 唐诗 (pronounced: táng shī)" and "song ci/ 宋词 (pronounced: sòng cí)".

Classical Chinese poetry has robust rules that draw attention to metres, level tones/ 平 (pronounced: píng), oblique tones/ 仄 (pronounced: zè), and rhymes. In the Middle Chinese language, there are four tone patterns/categories including: 1) level/ 平 (pronounced: píng); 2) rising/ 上 (pronounced: shǎng); 3) departing/ 去 (pronounced: qù); and 4) entering/ 入 (pronounced: rù), while Modern Standard Chinese does not have an "entering" pattern.

The four tones in Pinyin are primarily generated from the three tone patterns including: 1) level/ 平 (pronounced: píng); 2) rising/ 上 (pronounced: shǎng);

and 3) departing/ 去 (pronounced: qù). Noticeably, the first category of "level" is divided into "negative level/ 阴平 (pronounced: yīn píng)" and "positive level/ 阳平 (pronounced: yáng píng)" in modern Pinyin system. The full four tones in Pinyin are formulated as the first tone (tāng/ 汤), the second tone (táng/ 糖), the third tone (tǎng/ 躺), and the fourth tone (tàng/ 烫).

One key thing to keep in mind is that the tone category of entering/ 入 (pronounced: rù) does not exist in modern spoken Mandarin, yet can be found in dialects in some southern regions of China. Interestingly, many famous poets in the Tang and Song dynasties were from southern China, so a great amount of vocabulary using the entering tone pattern can be found in their poems. This explains why many Chinese-language learners may notice that some words and phrases do not conform to the principles of level and oblique tones (and even fail to rhyme) when reading those poems in Mandarin.

Here are two pieces of poetry, including one shi and

one ci that I personally appreciate very much.

将进酒

qiāng jìn jiǔ

李白

Li Bai

君不见，黄河之水天上来，奔流到海不复回。

jūn bù jiàn, huáng hé zhī shuǐ tiānshàng lái,

bēnliú dào hǎi bù fù huí.

君不见，高堂明镜悲白发，朝如青丝暮成雪。

jūn bù jiàn, gāotáng míngjìng bēi báifà,

zhāo rú qīngsī mù chéng xuě.

人生得意须尽欢，莫使金樽空对月。

rénshēng déyì xū jìn huān, mò shǐ jīnzūn kōng duì yuè.

天生我材必有用，千金散尽还复来。

tiān shēng wǒ cái bì yǒu yòng, qiān jīn sàn jìn huán fù lái.

烹羊宰牛且为乐，会须一饮三百杯。

pēng yáng zǎi niú qiě wéi lè, huì xū yī yǐn sānbǎi bēi.

岑夫子，丹丘生，将进酒，杯莫停。

cén fū zǐ, dān qiū shēng, qiāng jìn jiǔ, bēi mò tíng.

与君歌一曲，请君为我倾耳听。

yǔ jūn gē yī qǔ, qǐng jūn wèi wǒ cè ěr tīng.

钟鼓馔玉不足贵，但愿长醉不复醒。

zhōng gǔ zhuàn yù bù zú guì, dàn yuàn cháng zuì bù fù xǐng.

古来圣贤皆寂寞，惟有饮者留其名。

gǔ lái shèngxián jiē jìmò, wéi yǒu yǐn zhě liú qí míng.

陈王昔时宴平乐，斗酒十千恣欢谑。

chén wáng xī shí yàn píng lè, dǒu jiǔ shí qiān zì huānxuè.

主人何为言少钱，径须沽取对君酌。

zhǔ rén hé wèi yán shǎo qián, jìng xū gū qǔ duì jūn zhuó.

五花马，千金裘，

wǔ huā mǎ, qiān jīn qiú,

呼儿将出换美酒，与尔同销万古愁。

hū ér jiāng chū huàn měi jiǔ, yǔ ěr tóng xiāo wàn gǔ chóu.

Li Bai: Courtesy name Taibai; Art name Qinglian

Jushi.

Li Bai was the most representative figure of the Chinese Romantic Poetry School. Many of his poems have been handed down through generations, and a number of them have been honoured as poetic masterpieces. Li Bai was a genius poet, who loved drinking, and thus he is also designated as the "Poet Saint" and "Wine Immortal".

一剪梅

yī jiǎn méi

李清照

Li Qingzhao

红藕香残玉簟秋，轻解罗裳，独上兰舟。

云中谁寄锦书来？雁字回时，月满西楼。

hóng ǒu xiāng cán yù diàn qiū, qīng jiě luó cháng, dú shàng lán zhōu.

yún zhōng shuí jì jǐn shū lái? yàn zì huí shí, yuè mǎn xī lóu.

花自飘零水自流，一种相思，两处闲愁。

此情无计可消除，才下眉头，却上心头。

huā zì piāolíng shuǐ zì liú, yī zhǒng xiāng sī, liǎng chù xián chóu.

cǐ qíng wú jì kě xiāochú, cái xià méi tóu, què shàng xīn tóu.

Li Qingzhao: Art name Yi'an Jushi.

Li Qingzhao was an eminent female poet in the Song Dynasty and a representative figure of the Chinese Graceful and Restrained School. Li Qingzhao's life was very turbulent. While she felt contented and blissful with her husband Zhao Mingcheng in the first half of her life, she lived almost entirely in exile due to a collapse of both the country and her marriage.

Application

Please use the internet to explore the translated versions of the two poems I shared. See if you have captured the meaning explicitly. In addition, if you are passionate about poetry, I would like to recommend an app called "XuetangX", where you can find a vast collection of high-quality courses uploaded by prestigious universities in China – a lot of them are free of charge!

I have already studied a course via XuetangX: "The Appreciation of Tang and Song Poetry" taught by Professor Wang Bugao of Tsinghua University. The inspiring and informative lectures have expanded my knowledge and broadened my horizons. Therefore, I intended to write a letter in homage to Professor Wang. Unfortunately, I was informed that he had passed away. Hereby, through the publication of this book, I would like to express my deepest gratitude and condolences to the mentor that I never met!

Reflection

Chinese poets usually express their will or feelings in a condensed way. Can you think of whether there are any poets in your own country who you particularly like or admire? Are there any poems that you can easily recall? If so, grab a pen and write them down in your notebook.

If you have a general understanding of Chinese poetry, please also try to find out the differences between Chinese and western poets in terms of their language use and emotional expression.

第五章　中国书法

知识构建 / 应用实践 / 思考感想

知识构建

　　中国汉字博大精深，字体经历了数千年的进化和演变。书法在楷书的基础上形成的"草、行、隶、篆"，如同优美的舞蹈语汇，不同的形体，勾勒出不同的造型，把中国汉字结构的美展示到极致！能把书写变成书写艺术，在世界所有的文字中大概只有中国文字具备这种伸展空间，因此书法也被称为线条艺术。

　　中国书法大致分为五种书体：（1）楷书，（2）草书，（3）行书，（4）隶书，（5）篆书。其中，楷书尤为贴近现代书写形态，同时也是学习书法者首练的基本功。楷书中又有不同分类。欧阳询的欧体方正；颜真卿的颜体丰腴；柳公权的柳体劲瘦；赵孟頫的赵体秀逸。欧阳询、颜真卿、柳公权和赵孟頫被称为"楷书四大家"。我在这里给感兴趣的朋友推荐几张字帖[1]，大家可以自行品鉴。

写书法需要文房四宝[2]：毛笔、墨、砚台和宣纸。毛笔根据大小以及笔头用毛有不同的区分方式。毛笔的毛多是来自动物，按照其软硬程度可以分为"硬毫""软毫"等。墨是固体的墨和液体的墨汁的统称。墨汁可以直接用于书写，但如果是固体的墨条或墨块则需要砚台来研墨。传统宣纸的制作过程极为复杂，有超过百道工序之说。根据其吸水能力可以分为"熟宣""半熟宣""生宣"。熟宣纸质相对较硬，因此吸水能力较弱；生宣反之；半熟宣则介于二者之间。因此并不是熟宣就好过生宣，而是根据书写者的写作意图不同各取所需罢了。

---

1 见 84—87 页图。
2 见 88 页图。

应用实践

领略了中国书法之美后你现在是不是有种跃跃欲试的冲动？请在下面的字格里先临摹一下，小试牛刀吧。有几个简单的口诀供大家参考：

握笔姿势：

指实掌虚，

腕平掌竖。

书写时：

提中有按，按中有提。

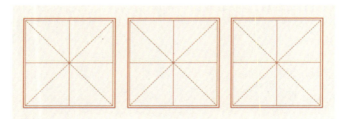

思考感想

看过了不同的书写体，你最感兴趣的是哪种？为什么？

之前提到过的"楷书四大家"其中三位都是唐代人，可以试想一下为什么书法（楷书）在唐代如此盛行？可结合第四章内容进行思考。

九成宮醴泉銘
祕書監撿挍侍
中鉅鹿郡公臣
魏徵奉　勅撰

山抗殿絕壑為池
跨水架楹分巖竦
闕高閣周建長廊
四起棟宇膠葛臺

欧阳询《九成宫醴泉铭》
Ouyang Xun

岳瀆之秀冰雪之姿
果屑貝齒蓮目月面
望之屬即之溫觀相
未言而降伏之心已
過半矣同行禪師抱

颜真卿《多宝塔碑》
Yan Zhenqing

悟禪師為沙弥十七正度為比丘緣安國寺具威儀於西明寺

柳公权《玄秘塔碑》
Liu Gongquan

赵孟頫《湖州妙严寺记》
Zhao Mengfu

文房四宝

Four Treasures of the Study

Chapter 5: Chinese Calligraphy/ 中国书法

(pronounced: zhōngguó shūfǎ)

Construction

A broad range of Chinese characters and their fonts have undergone thousands of years of transformation and evolution. Based on regular script/ 楷书 (pronounced: kǎi shū), Chinese script styles have developed into cursive script/ 草书 (pronounced: cǎo shū), semi-cursive script/ 行书 (pronounced: xíng shū), clerical script/ 隶书 (pronounced: lì shū), and seal script/ 篆书 (pronounced: zhuàn shū). Like a language conveyed by a beautiful dance, various scripts delineate different bodies, all of which demonstrate the structural beauty of Chinese characters to the extreme! Chinese characters are probably the only kind in the world with the spatial ability for extension and expansion. Therefore, Chinese calligraphy is also regarded as the art of brushstrokes.

As mentioned, there are five major scripts in Chinese calligraphy: 1) regular script; 2) cursive script; 3) semi-cursive script; 4) clerical script; and 5) seal script. Among them, regular script is particularly close to the modern writing form and knowing how to write correctly with regular script is also considered a fundamental skill for people learning calligraphy. Regular script has four main styles: Ou, Yan, Liu, and Zhao. Ou/ 欧 (pronounced: ōu) style was created by Ouyang Xun and features grandness; Yan/ 颜 (pronounced: yán) style was developed by Yan Zhenqing and thrives on boldness; Liu Gongquan's Liu/ 柳 (pronounced: liǔ) style tends to be slender; and Zhao Mengfu's Zhao/ 赵 (pronounced: zhào) style is flowing. I have only studied calligraphy for a short period and am still just a novice, so I dare not judge the works of the four masters of regular script. Instead, I would like to recommend a few calligraphy copybooks[1] that you might want to read and use.

The ink brush, ink, inkstone, and paper are considered necessities for Chinese calligraphy, and all of these instruments are referred to as the Four Treasures of the Study[2]/ 文房四宝 (pronounced: wén fáng sì bǎo). Brushes are classified differently according to size and texture. Brush heads are mainly made from animal hair and can have various degrees of softness or hardness, such as the hard-hair brush/ 硬毫 (pronounced: yìng háo), the soft-hair brush/ 软毫 (pronounced: ruǎn háo), and the mixed-hair brush/ 兼毫 (pronounced: jiān háo).

Ink is the general term for a solid ink stick and liquid ink. Liquid ink can be used directly for writing, while solid ink sticks must be ground on an inkstone

1 See pictures on pages 84-87.
2 See picture on page 88.

first. A special paper called Xuanzhi/ 宣纸 (pronounced: xuān zhǐ) is believed to best fit Chinese calligraphy. The production process of such paper is very complicated, and it is said that there are over 100 procedures to follow in its creation. Paper can be classified according to its water absorption capacity – "ripe xuan/ 熟宣 (pronounced: shú xuān)", "half-ripe xuan/ 半熟宣 (pronounced: bàn shú xuān)", and "raw xuan/ 生宣 (pronounced: shēng xuān)". Ripe xuan is relatively stiff, so it lacks the ability to absorb water. Raw xuan is the opposite, while half-ripe xuan sits in the middle. One paper type is not better than another and its use comes down to the writer's preference.

Application

From sensing the beauty of Chinese calligraphy, are you keen on trying it yourself? Please imitate writing a few characters in the following grids. Here are a couple of tips.

Brush grasp:

Fingers: to push pressure on the body of the brush

Palm: not to touch anything

Wrist: to keep flat

Palm: to keep vertical

When writing:

Try to strike a finely tuned balance between push and pull the brush

Reflection

After viewing the different script types, which one did you find most interesting and inspiring? Why?

Three out of the four great calligraphers who specialised in regular script mentioned earlier lived in the Tang Dynasty. Please consider why calligraphy (regular script) was so far-reaching in that period. You can also refer to what you have read in Chapter 4 to answer this question.

第六章　中国京剧

知识构建 / 应用实践 / 思考感想

知识构建

　　京剧被誉为中国的国粹。京剧的盛行源于清代皇室的追捧，但在当代随着其他娱乐形式的产生，真正听戏看戏的人少之又少。

　　在我的记忆中，我的祖母是个十足的戏迷。那时正值改革开放初期，家里刚刚有了电视机。祖母闲暇时间除玩花牌以外，基本都用在听戏上。由于耳濡目染，小时候的我居然会唱几段京剧名段，例如《四郎探母》《甘露寺》《沙家浜》中的唱段。

京剧里的角色¹主要分为"生""旦""净""丑"。其中，"旦"和"丑"比较好理解。"旦"通指女性角色，而"丑"则指滑稽幽默的角色，和外国文艺中的"小丑"有异曲同工之妙。"生"多指正面男性角色，"净"则是性格豪迈、粗犷的男性的代名词。有人将"生"单一地理解为是文弱的书生，其实不然。"生"中也有武生这一行当。一个比较简单的区分"生"和"净"的方式是脸谱。

"净"的特点表现在脸谱——花脸²。花脸的颜色极为讲究。其中红色代表刚正不阿，白色代表奸诈狡猾。中国有句俗话：一个唱红脸，一个唱白脸。这里的"红脸"是正面角色，即好人；"白脸"是反面角色，即坏人。这句俗语的意思是讲求分工合作来达成某种共有的目的。举个简单的例子：中国的父母通常在教育孩子问题上一个唱红脸，一个唱白脸。进一步来解释，父母在教育孩子的目标上基本一致。为了不给孩子施加太多压力，一位会比较严厉，另一位则是和风细雨。在孩子的眼中，"好人"和"坏人"不言而喻。

---

1 见 101 页图。
2 见 102 页图。

应用实践

1993 年的中国春节联欢晚会上，一首与流行音乐相结合的《说唱脸谱》通俗易懂，脍炙人口。其中有段歌词为"红脸的关公……白脸的曹操"。结合我在上文中提到的脸谱的颜色，思考一下这两位历史人物的性格特点吧。

《说唱脸谱》的试听链接：

https://www.youtube.com/watch?v=3ADkOwJgawQ

另外，通过歌曲来进行语言的深化学习已经被许多语言学家反复印证为非常有效的方法。以我个人经验为例，我当初选择学习韩语是源于一个特别简单的理由——为了能唱韩语歌。而我又把每天从欣赏不同类型的韩语歌曲中获得的愉悦感转化为源源不绝的动力，从而进一步增加了我对学习该语言的乐趣。于是，在学习了韩语大约半年左右后，我不仅能唱韩语歌，而且还通过了韩语 TOPIK 的中级考试。值得一提的是，我后来的两次韩国之旅都是自由行。在这个过程中，我成功地把学习到的语言进行了实战的运用，更增添了我学习韩语的信心。

如果你也同样热爱音乐，找几首你喜欢的中文歌，或是自己哼唱，或是约三五好友一起到 KTV 嗨起来吧。

思考感想

如果此章引发了你对中国京剧的兴趣，建议你通过网络了解京剧的鼻祖程长庚何时带领"徽剧"戏班进京，以至后来形成的"安徽人演、北京人看、上海人命名"的京剧演变过程。二百余年的中国京剧发展史，相信一定会引起你极大的兴趣！

另外，越剧作为中国第二大戏曲剧种，因其曲调优美，也广受观众喜爱。越剧起源于江浙地区，先盛行于中国南方，后渐渐被其他地区观众所接受。因此，越剧被称为"流传最广的地方剧种"。说到越剧的代表剧目，古装戏《梁山伯与祝英台》无疑是首选。此剧源于民间传说：祝英台女扮男装在求学期间结识同窗梁山伯，无奈因家人阻挠，无法结成良缘，最终双双饮恨而终。这凄美的爱情故事中也暗含了中国封建社会女性地位的弱势以及森严的宗法制度。因此也有学者把其称为东方版的《罗密欧与朱丽叶》。

越剧《梁山伯与祝英台》试看链接：

https://www.youtube.com/watch?v=Ff0T3O9UHxg

结合自己的品位和喜好，看看你是更喜欢京剧还是越剧？如果有兴趣的话，也请利用网络搜索一下中国其他的地方剧种，说不定也会有意外发现哦。

京剧剧照

Peking Opera

京剧剧照

Painted Face Roles

Chapter 6: Peking Opera/ 中国京剧

(pronounced: zhōngguó jīng jù)

Construction

Peking Opera/ 京剧 (pronounced: jīng jù) is reputed as the quintessence of China. The popularity of Peking Opera was propelled by the imperial royal and nobility in the Qing Dynasty. However, with the emergence of other forms of entertainment in modern times, Chinese people, especially younger people, have lost their appetite for this traditional art form.

When recollecting my childhood, I remember that my grandmother was a huge fan of Peking Opera. In the early stages of China's reform and opening-up, my family could finally afford a home television. In addition to playing her favourite card game — Mahjong, my grandmother spent the rest of her spare time watching Peking Operas on television. Being imbued with what I had seen and heard alongside my grandmother, I could even sing several famous Peking Opera excerpts, such as *Silang Visits His Mother, Ganlu Temple*, and *Shajiabang — Wisdom Fight*.

The roles in Peking Opera[1] mainly consist of Sheng/ 生 (pronounced: shēng), Dan/ 旦 (pronounced: dàn), Jing/ 净 (pronounced: jìng), and Chou/ 丑 (pronounced: chǒu). Among these, Dan and Chou can be explained easily, as Dan generally refers to female characters, while Chou signifies comedic roles, similar to clowns in western drama. Sheng mainly represents decent male characters, while Jing can be considered synonymous with bold and rugged men. Some people may interpret Sheng as

---

1 See picture on page 101.

a vulnerable scholar, but this is not true. Sheng also includes male roles who are good at martial arts, which is called Wu Sheng/ 武生 (pronounced: wǔ shēng). A simple way to distinguish between Sheng and Jing is their face paint.

Jing is also regarded as a painted face role[1] – Hualian/ 花脸 (pronounced: huā liǎn) and the face colour is very particular. For example, red represents uprightness and loyalty, while white means cunning and villainous. There is a saying in China – "One performs a red face, while the other wears a white face". The "red face" is likened to the good person drawn from the well-known negotiation strategy of "good cop, bad cop", while the "white face" is likened to the bad cop. Similarly, this Chinese proverb implies that the division of two different conflicting roles can help achieve a common goal.

Interestingly, Chinese parents usually perform the

---

1   See picture on page 102.

red face and the white face tactic for their children's education. For example, one parent can be gentle or indulgent, while the other will be strict. This is because many Chinese parents often attach great importance to their children's academic performance but do not want to smother their children.

Application

At the Chinese Spring Festival Gala in 1993, a song called Shuo Chang Lian Pu/ 说唱脸谱 (pronounced: shuō chàng liǎn pǔ) combined Peking Opera with popular music. The lyrics conveyed the essence of face painting in Peking Opera in a colloquial way. One line of the lyrics was, "red-faced Guan Gong (also known as Guan Yu) ...white-faced Cao Cao". After reading about the meaning of the colours of the face paint mentioned above, you may wish to guess what the personalities were of these two historical figures of the Three Kingdoms.

Shuo Chang Lian Pu YouTube link:

https://www.youtube.com/watch?v=3ADkOwJgawQ

Many linguists have repeatedly identified and proven that intensifying language learning through songs and music is very effective. For example, I chose to study the Korean language for a very simple reason – to sing Korean songs. My motivation was always high throughout the learning process, which increased my enjoyment of learning Korean. As a result, after studying Korean for just half a year, I could not only sing Korean songs, but also passed the TOPIK intermediate-level test. Furthermore, my two trips to South Korea were self-guided tours, and the language skills I learned were applied in real-life settings. In turn, these practical experiences have enhanced my confidence when using the Korean language.

If you also love music and songs, you can try to find several Chinese songs that you like. Then, hum them to yourself or go to KTV with a bunch of friends to have fun together.

Reflection

If the content of this chapter stimulates your interest in Peking Opera, I suggest you trace the origin of this traditional art form via the internet. For example, you could explore when Cheng Changgeng, the pioneer of Peking Opera, navigated the "Hui opera" troupe to Beijing and later led the evolution of the opera. There are over 200 years of developmental history of Peking Opera to enjoy, and it is very informative and stimulating, which I hope will ring your bell and inspire you to do more research by yourself.

In addition, Yue opera/ 越剧 (pronounced: yuè jù),

the second-largest genre of operas in China, is also fascinating because of its beautiful tunes. Yue opera originated in the Jiangsu and Zhejiang regions, was first popular in southern China, and was gradually admired by audiences in other regions. Yue opera is therefore regarded as the most widely performed local opera. As for the repertoire of Yue opera, *Butterfly Lovers* (also known as *Liang Shanbo and Zhu Yingtai*) must rank highly. Originating from folklore, the story goes that Zhu Yingtai disguised herself as a male and met her classmate Liang Shanbo during her studies. However, she could not marry him due to severe objections from her family. Eventually, both died in despair and hopelessness. This poignant love story also speaks of the disadvantaged status of women in China's feudal society and the strict patriarchal system. For this reason, some scholars refer to it as the oriental version of *Romeo and Juliet*.

Butterfly Lovers YouTube link:
https://www.youtube.com/watch?v=Ff0T3O9UHxg

Do you prefer Peking Opera or Yue opera based on your own tastes and preferences? If this traditional art form charms you, you can use the internet to search for other local operas in China, and I hope you may find serendipity!

第七章　中国相声

知识构建 / 应用实践 / 思考感想

知识构建

　　文化历来有雅俗之分。一提到俗文化很容易让人想到低俗、粗糙、不堪。其实这是一种偏见。有史以来，文化的分野是由特定人群的不同取舍而形成的。俗话说"萝卜白菜，各有所爱"。能引发观众自觉地进行哲理性思考的作品是文艺，看了让观众捧腹大笑、缓解疲劳的作品同样也是文艺。以此非彼或以彼非此都是错误的。俗文化往往更贴近人间烟火、更接地气，因此受众面更广。中国的相声就属于最受普罗大众喜爱的俗文化里的一种艺术形式。

　　相声是一门传统的语言艺术，初现于清代年间。相声，音同"像生"，意指模仿他人的言行举止。相声的初期形态多为单人模仿口技。后期逐渐发展为大家所更为熟悉的对口（双人）相声以及群口（多人）相声。

估计当下很多人谈到单口相声，首先想到的还是马三立先生的经典小段《逗你玩》。这位相声界的泰斗在他短短几分钟的作品里融入了方言以及对他人行动上的模仿，使得整个表演十分生动，频频逗趣儿。熟悉相声的朋友都知道，相声的四门功课分别是"说""学""逗""唱"。在马三立先生的上述作品中，他除"唱"（太平歌词）没有展现之外，其他三门技艺可谓发挥得淋漓尽致。

《逗你玩》的试看链接：

https://www.youtube.com/watch?v=ul7K2S2fX5s

值得思考的是，为什么相声这种传统的艺术形式在当代还能被很多年轻人所喜爱？我能想到的原因之一是：它可以紧跟时代的脚步。四门功课中，除"唱"之外，其他三样皆可与现代元素相结合来迎合观众口味的改变。比如演员们可以"说"一些现代年轻人喜欢的梗，"学"一些大众喜欢的流行歌曲等。这与上一章节谈到的京剧是截然不同的。

对口 [1] 是目前相声的主流形式，两位演员往台上一站，一逗一捧，分工明确，相得益彰。负责主要逗笑的演员被称为"逗哏"。值得一提的是，这里的"哏"指的是段子中的笑点或笑料。负责烘托或者铺垫气氛的则被称为"捧哏"。不少刚接触相声的观众会下意识认为"逗哏"的词较多而且有趣，所以"逗哏"想当然是主角。但我认为一段相声之所以能够成功，"捧哏"对现场气氛的拿捏自然也是功不可没的。这里给大家介绍一对我个人非常喜欢的"神仙组合"——郭德纲和于谦。大家有空可以去应用程序"喜马拉雅"搜搜这两位相声大家的经典段子来听听，既能愉悦自己的心情，也能学习到正宗的京腔，可谓是一举两得。

另外，如果大家有机会，强烈建议去听听德云社相声的现场版（注：德云社是郭德纲在 1995 年创立的相声社团）。我有幸在中国北京和新西兰奥克兰听了两场，觉得十分值回票价。

1　见 117 页图。

应用实践

上面谈到的相声演员的四门功课中，"说"是排在首位的。在这个基本功的培养过程中，其中一个重点便是训练演员们的口齿伶俐。绕口令自然而然成为他们练习咬字以及发音声调的不二法门。

犹记得我上中学时，曾较为系统地学习过表演课程。为了发音的字正腔圆，也是每天下苦功练习绕口令。凭借记忆中的碎片，分享几个给大家。

- 吃葡萄不吐葡萄皮，不吃葡萄倒吐葡萄皮。
- 八百标兵奔北坡，炮兵并排北边跑，炮兵怕把标兵碰，标兵怕碰炮兵炮。
- 有个小孩叫小杜，上街打醋又买布。买了布，打了醋，回头看见鹰抓兔。放下布，搁下醋，上前去追鹰和兔，飞了鹰，跑了兔，洒了醋，湿了布。

大家如果对这样的句子感兴趣，可以自行上网搜索更多的绕口令来练习。通过训练嘴巴和口腔的肌肉记忆，尽早来征服汉语发音吧。

思考感想

　　想一想在自己的国家里，有哪些传统的艺术形式为了适应
时代的发展而作出了改变？你喜欢这种改变吗？为什么？

相声漫画

作者：吕晨

Crosstalk Characters

By Lyu Chen

Chapter 7: Chinese Crosstalk/ 中国相声

(pronounced: zhōngguó xiàngsheng)

Construction

Culture has been described as both elegant and vulgar, and no one culture seems exempt from this. When it comes to vulgarity, people tend to think of language or art forms that are coarse, uncouth, and unrefined. In fact, this could be considered prejudicial! In my opinion, the dichotomy between cultural superiority and inferiority is actually a product of a power hierarchy created by different specific groups of people.

As the Chinese saying goes, "萝卜白菜，各有所爱 (pronounced: luó bo bái cài, gè yǒu suǒ ài)" – there are different strokes for different folks. From my perspective, works that can inspire an audience to rationally and consciously ponder the underlying meanings can be great pieces of literature and art, while works that can amuse the audience and relieve fatigue can also be considered great pieces. Therefore, one cannot be better than another. Folk culture is often attached to people's real lives and is more down-to-earth, thus appealing to a wider audience. Chinese crosstalk is one of the most popular art forms representing folk culture.

Crosstalk is a traditional language art that first appeared during the Qing Dynasty. Crosstalk/ 相声 (pronounced: xiàng sheng), has the homophone of xiang sheng/ 像生 , which means imitating the words and actions of others. The initial form of crosstalk was similar to a monologue – a single person performing ventriloquism. Later, it gradually developed into other forms such as a dialogue between two actors or a group act performed by three people or more.

The first classic monologue excerpt that most audiences could name is probably Mr Ma Sanli's *Just Kidding*. This master of crosstalk has incorporated dialects and imitations of different people, such as a sneaky thief, an overwhelmed housewife, and a naive child, into this a-few-minute-performances, making his whole act vivid and amusing. You have probably heard that the four skills of crosstalk include speaking, imitating, teasing, and singing. In Mr Ma Sanli's act, he showed three out of four skills expertly: speaking, imitating, and teasing.

Just Kidding YouTube link:

https://www.youtube.com/watch?v=ul7K2S2fX5s

It is worth reflecting on why many young people in contemporary society still appreciate this traditional art form. One of the reasons that I can point out is that it can keep abreast of the times. Among the four skills mentioned earlier, except for singing, the other three can be adapted with novel elements threaded in to cater to modern audiences' changing tastes. For example, actors can talk about punchlines of jokes that young people like and learn some popular songs that fit recent trends. In contrast, another traditional art form – Peking opera, obviously lacks the flexibility to do so.

A dialogue between two actors[1] is presently the mainstream form of crosstalk. The two performers stand on the stage, with one being the wisecracker and the other being the stooge. The division of performing tasks is clear. The actor in charge of amusing the audience is called dougen/ 逗哏 (pronounced: dòu gén), the wisecracker in English. Gen/ 哏 (pronounced: gén) here refers to the core part of jokes. The performer who helps set off the context and lights up the atmosphere is called penggen/ 捧哏 (pronounced: pěng gén), the stooge in English.

---

1 See picture on page 117.

People who are new to such an art form may subconsciously think that dougen must be the leading actor, because he has got most of the punchlines and has the main responsibility to amuse the audience. I, however, believe that the success of a crosstalk act should also be attributed to a good penggen, who supports dougen all the time. Without penggen's response, the show will turn into a soliloquy or even lull the audience to sleep. Here I would like to introduce two masters of Chinese crosstalk: Guo Degang/ 郭德纲 and Yu Qian/ 于谦, who always complement each other during their performance, and are thus nicknamed the "immortal combination".

If you are interested in crosstalk, you can download an app called "Himalaya" and search for some excerpts to listen. Crosstalk can not only bring you pleasure, but also serve as an excellent opportunity for you to learn the authentic Beijing accent. You can kill two birds with one stone.

By the way, if you have the opportunity, I would strongly recommend you to go to De Yun She/ 德云社 (pronounced: dé yún shè) and enjoy the crosstalk live (Note: De Yun She is a crosstalk club founded by Guo Degang in 1995). I watched two shows in Beijing, China, and Auckland, New Zealand, and I thought they were totally worth the price.

Application

Among the four skills of crosstalk actors, "speaking" comes first and foremost. When cultivating this skill, the key principle is to train the actors to be articulate. Tongue twister practice is one of the most effective ways for actors to hone their skills in pronunciation and articulation.

When I was in middle school, I used to take acting classes. I still remember I worked so hard on practising tongue twisters every morning so that my pronunciation could sound faultless. Here are some examples:

⊙ 吃葡萄不吐葡萄皮，不吃葡萄倒吐葡萄皮。

chī pútáo bù tǔ pútáo pí, bù chī pútáo dào tǔ pútáo pí.

⊙ 八百标兵奔北坡，炮兵并排北边跑，炮兵怕把标兵碰，标兵怕碰炮兵炮。

bā bǎi biāo bīng bèn běi pō, pào bīng bìng pái běi biān pǎo, pào bīng pà bǎ biāo bīng pèng, biāo bīng pà pèng pào bīng pào.

⊙ 有个小孩叫小杜，上街打醋又买布。买了布，打了醋，回头看见鹰抓兔。放下布，搁下醋，上前去追鹰和兔，飞了鹰，跑了兔，洒了醋，湿了布。

yǒu gè xiǎo hái jiào xiǎo dù, shàng jiē dǎ cù yòu mǎi bù. mǎi le bù, dǎ le cù, huí tóu kàn jiàn yīng zhuā tù. fàng xià bù, gē xià cù, shàng qián qù zhuī yīng hé tù, fēi le yīng, pǎo le tù, sǎ le cù, shī le bù.

If you feel interested in such practices, you can

search for more tongue twisters online and try them yourself! Train your speech muscles and then build muscle memory so that hopefully, you can conquer the Chinese pronunciation challenge one day.

Reflection

Please examine what traditional art forms in your own country have changed in order to keep pace with the development of the times. Do you like the changes? Why?

茉莉之屋
Jasmine's House

第八章　中国园林

知识构建 / 应用实践 / 思考感想

知识构建

　　我的父亲是位影、视、剧三栖演员，因为职业的方便，他每到一地都要游览当地古老且有特色的建筑。他说那些看似破旧的物体实际却承载着百年甚至千年的文化。受父亲的影响，我每次旅行也都把精力放在寻觅当地遗留下来的古老建筑中，着实获益匪浅。

　　我早年留学欧洲，在那里有幸接触到了不同历史时期的建筑文化遗产。其中印象较为深刻的是巴洛克建筑风格与哥特式建筑风格有趣的融合。这种看似不协调的美恰恰反映出 17 世纪欧洲大陆迥异的思潮碰撞。中国，作为千年古国，自然也有其独具一格的建筑。谈到中国的建筑特色，就不得不说说中国的园林。

园林，乍一听很容易理解为"植物园""国家森林公园"之类，实则不然。中国园林是对中国民间独具中国传统建筑美学的私人建筑群的总称。中国园林艺术讲究人工与自然交融之美。运用亭阁、廊柱、水榭等中国传统建筑元素和符号既使得局部独立成景，也符合于整体的需要。中国园林可大致分为皇家园林和私家园林。前者顾名思义是为古代帝王所打造，代表园林为地处北京的颐和园。后者则为官宦和富商所拥有，代表园林为地处苏州的拙政园。

与皇家园林相比，我个人更喜欢私家园林。皇家园林大而奢华，皇亲国戚游览需骑马乘轿。如徒步游览，兴致极易被疲劳冲淡。而私人园林则更人性化：小巧紧凑，移步即景。使得游人充满享受感。其中拙政园[1]作为江南古典园林代表，更是深得我心。像之前提到过的，建筑本身虽然是静态化的物体，但是却承载着风霜岁月，背后的故事往往令人唏嘘。例如中国绍兴的"沈园"，宋代著名诗人陆游与他钟爱的前妻分手多年后竟在"沈园"里邂逅，悲伤痛惜之余当即写下一首忏悔词

1　见 132 页图。

《钗头凤》。这段流传千古的凄美爱情故事，每年吸引着成千上万的国内外游客前往。由于历史悠久，可以说每一座中国园林都会诉说一段精彩故事，拙政园同样也不例外。拙政园原由明代大臣王献臣所建。因仕途凶险，王献臣辞官还乡后花数年打造此园。据传他还请自己的至交好友，江南四大才子之一的文徵明来参与设计。无奈造化弄人，园子建好没多久，王献臣因病辞世。其子不知长进，一夜豪赌，竟把整个园子输与旁人。后辗转于多名买家之手，频繁易主。

现拙政园拓展为约 5.2 公顷，大致分为东、中、西三个部分。拙政园内部巧妙地运用了人工元素，例如水池、假山、亭廊、水榭和谐有致地坐落在林柏花丛之间。拙政园的妙处在于移步易景，随着游客脚踪的变化，景观也在不时地转换。

在这里附上我父亲游拙政园后写的诗，与大家共享。

游拙政园

王虎城

半顷空间无地闲，亭廊水榭阁齐全。

举目四顾皆为景，出了拙政不看园。

应用实践

请大家找一张纸，尝试着在上面画一幢具有自己国家风格的建筑物吧。同时也请思考一下其背后的文化及历史。

找来自己身边的中国朋友，给他们讲讲自己国家有代表性的建筑吧。记得加入一些历史故事情节，会更加引人入胜哦。

思考感想

现如今，很多建筑的构建牺牲了其艺术特性，更多地注重其作用及目的。你认同这样的改变吗？

拙政园

The Humble Administrator's Garden

Chapter 8: Chinese Gardens/ 中国园林

(pronounced: zhōngguó yuán lín)

Construction

My father is an actor and has dedicated his career to films, television, and the stage. He always travels so that he can work on location. My father sees travelling as a bonus instead of a burden, because he loves visiting ancient and iconic buildings of different places wherever he goes. He usually proclaims that archaic or dilapidated objects have embodied hundreds or even thousands of years of culture and history. I am influenced by my father's ideas. Every time I travel, I invest my energy and time seeking out local heritage buildings from which I find much inspiration.

I studied at a university in Europe many years ago, where I was fortunate enough to be exposed to a wide variety of architectural heritage from many different historical periods. One of the most impressive was the fascinating fusion of Baroque and Gothic architectural styles. The incongruous splendour reflects the collision and confluence of various ideological trends in the European continent in the 17th century. China, with thousands of years of history has its own unique architectural qualities. When it comes to Chinese architecture, Chinese gardens cannot be disregarded.

Gardens, at first glance, could be misunderstood as "botanical gardens" or "national forest parks", but this is not what Chinese gardens refer to. The Chinese garden is a general term for a private estate that embodies unique Chinese traditional architectural aesthetics. Chinese garden art draws attention to the beauty of blending the artificial and natural. Traditional Chinese architectural elements and structures, such as halls, galleries, pavilions, and ponds can be independently outstanding while remaining harmonious with the entire garden. The subtlety of the Chinese garden design enables visitors to see a series of scenes from different points of view.

Chinese gardens can be categorised into royal gardens and private gardens. As its name suggests, the former was built for ancient emperors and the imperial family. An example of such kind of garden is Summer Palace in Beijing. Officials and wealthy businessmen owned the latter, with the Humble Administrator's Garden in Suzhou being one example.

I personally prefer private gardens to royal gardens. The royal garden is always vast and luxurious. Royal family members used to ride horses or sit in sedan chairs to go sightseeing, because exploring by foot could be fatiguing and affect their mood. Private gardens are relatively small and compact and are more accessible to people. As a visitor, you can view the scenery wherever you go, and this adds to your enjoyment. The Humble Administrator's Garden[1], for example, totally won my heart.

Despite the fact that the garden itself is a static object, the story behind it is often appealing, but sometimes heartbreaking. The Shen Garden in Shaoxing, Zhejiang province is an example of this. The prominent Song Dynasty poet Lu You and his beloved ex-wife crossed paths in the Shen Garden. Many years elapsed before they met again. While grieving, he wrote a poem of repentance called Chai Tou Feng/ 钗头凤 (pronounced: chāi tóu fèng). This poignant love story passed down through the ages attracts thousands of domestic and foreign tourists to visit the garden every year.

Due to their long histories, every Chinese garden, arguably, could tell a remarkable story. The Humble Administrator's Garden is no exception. The garden

---

1   See pictures on page 132.

was primarily built by Wang Xianchen, a minister of the Ming Dynasty. Due to his frustrating political career, Wang Xianchen disappointedly resigned from office and returned to his home town. He then devoted years to building and staging the garden. He also invited his friend, Wen Zhengming, who was one of the four great talents of the Ming Dynasty, to help plan the landscape and design the estate. Unfortunately, not long after the garden was built, Wang Xianchen died of illness. His son was ignorant and incompetent, obsessed with gambling, and finally lost the whole estate. The garden has since been passed through many hands.

The Humble Administrator's Garden has been expanded to approximately 5.2 hectares and is divided into three parts: east, middle, and west. The glamorous estate makes the most of artificial elements such as ponds, rockeries, halls, and water pavilions, all of which harmoniously complement each other and are well set in the backdrop of cypresses and flowers. When you wend your way through the garden, you may feel as though the series of scenes seem to follow your footsteps, which is the infinite attractiveness of the Humble Administrator's Garden.

Here is a poem that my father wrote after he visited the Humble Administrator's Garden:

游拙政园

yóu zhuó zhèng yuán

王虎城

Wang Hucheng

半顷空间无地闲，亭廊水榭阁齐全。

bàn qǐng kōngjiān wú dì xián, tíng láng shuǐ xiè gé qí quán.

举目四顾皆为景，出了拙政不看园。

jǔ mù sì gù jiē wéi jǐng, chū le zhuó zhèng bù kàn yuán.

The Humble Administrator's Garden Tour

A scroll of scenery unfurls:
Halls, galleries, waterside pavilions,
kiosks squatting in acres of space.
Leave the garden in despair
For the spaces vanished from there.

Application

Please take a piece of paper and try to draw buildings that bear your own country's architectural features and styles. Deliberate about the culture and history behind the buildings.

Please go to your Chinese friends and tell them about the iconic buildings in your country. Remember to add some historical storylines as this will sound more interesting.

Reflection

Today, many buildings are constructed at the expense of their artistic values and instead focus more on their function and purpose. Do you think such a change is positive?

附录——成语总结
Bonus — Idioms Summary

　　成语是汉语文化中不可或缺的一大要素。成语通常由四个汉字组成。这样的固定短语可以用来精简凝练地表达出自己的意思。许多成语背后亦有历史故事或者哲学思想作为支撑，因此成语也可以被看作中华民族文化的承载与体现。在此附录中，我总结了本书所有章节里出现的四字成语。请大家跟着读一读，写一写。如果时间充裕的话，也请利用手头的学习资源查一查该成语的意思，尝试更深入地去理解。亦可以利用我在本书中提出的一些语言学习的小技巧，把这些词真正纳入自己的知识库中，并在实践中有所运用。

　　Idioms/ 成语 (pronounced: chéng yǔ) play an indispensable role in Chinese language and culture. In

China, idioms are commonly presented in four Chinese characters. Such phrases can be concise and acute in helping express meanings. Many idioms have been framed and formed in the contexts of historical events or are supported by philosophical ideology. Because of this, idioms can also be seen as a carrier and embodiment of Chinese culture. This appendix summarises the four-character idioms that are noted in this book.

If you have adequate time, please make the most of the learning resources on hand to check the meaning of the idioms and understand them more in-depth. I would also encourage you to utilise some of the learning tips provided in this book, which I hope can help you effectively incorporate new learnings into your knowledge base for use in practical situations.

理所当然	八方支援
lǐ suǒ dāng rán	bā fāng zhī yuán
天经地义	保驾护航
tiān jīng dì yì	bǎo jià hù háng

历久弥新
lì jiǔ mí xīn

广为人知
guǎng wéi rén zhī

大开大合
dà kāi dà hé

别出心裁
bié chū xīn cái

原汁原味
yuán zhī yuán wèi

举一反三
jǔ yī fǎn sān

谈古论今
tán gǔ lùn jīn

芸芸众生
yún yún zhòng shēng

海阔天空
hǎi kuò tiān kōng

故弄玄虚
gù nòng xuán xū

脱颖而出
tuō yǐng ér chū

水涨船高
shuǐ zhǎng chuán gāo

名噪一时
míng zào yī shí

千古绝唱
qiān gǔ jué chàng

命运多舛
mìng yùn duō chuǎn

颠沛流离
diān pèi liú lí

受益匪浅
shòu yì fěi qiǎn

信手拈来
xìn shǒu niān lái

博大精深
bó dà jīng shēn

各取所需
gè qǔ suǒ xū

跃跃欲试
yuè yuè yù shì

小试牛刀
xiǎo shì niú dāo

耳濡目染	相得益彰
ěr rú mù rǎn	xiāng dé yì zhāng
异曲同工	一举两得
yì qǔ tóng gōng	yī jǔ liǎng dé
刚正不阿	自然而然
gāng zhèng bù ē	zì rán ér rán
不言而喻	不二法门
bù yán ér yù	bù èr fǎ mén
脍炙人口	字正腔圆
kuài zhì rén kǒu	zì zhèng qiāng yuán
源源不绝	独具一格
yuán yuán bù jué	dú jù yī gé
饮恨而终	顾名思义
yǐn hèn ér zhōng	gù míng sī yì
捧腹大笑	引人入胜
pěng fù dà xiào	yǐn rén rù shèng
淋漓尽致	流传千古
lín lí jìn zhì	liú chuán qiān gǔ
截然不同	造化弄人
jié rán bù tóng	zào huà nòng rén

参考文献
Bibliography

［1］孔子弟子及再传弟子 . 论语〔Ｍ〕. 北京：中华书局，2016.

［2］Maslow, A. H. A theory of human motivation〔J〕. Psychological
　　Review, 1943, 50(4): 370-396.

［3］吴杰、张亚琴 . 四大菜系常用菜谱精选〔Ｍ〕. 北京：农村
　　读物出版社 , 2000.

［4］詹伯慧 . 广州话正音字典〔Ｍ〕. 广州：广东人民出版社，2002.

［5］姚国坤、王存礼、程启坤 . 中国茶文化〔Ｍ〕. 上海：上海
　　文化出版社 , 1991.

［6］詹詹 . 一席茶：茶席设计与茶道美学〔Ｍ〕. 北京：中国轻
　　工业出版社 , 2019.

［7］徐秀棠 . 中国紫砂〔Ｍ〕. 上海：上海古籍出版社 , 2005.

［8］王虎城 . 虎城文影〔Ｍ〕. 北京：大众文艺出版社 , 2009.

［9］叶喆民．中国陶瓷史［M］．北京：生活·读书·新知三联书店，2011.

［10］李白．李白诗选［M］．香港：三联书店（香港）有限公司，2020.

［11］李清照．李清照诗词集［M］．上海：上海古籍出版社，2016.

［12］王步高．唐宋诗词鉴赏［M］．北京：北京大学出版社，2007.

［13］刘涛．极简中国书法史［M］．北京：人民美术出版社，2014.

［14］王正良．楷书四大家名碑临写指南［M］．西安：陕西人民美术出版社，2000.

［15］齐儆．中国的文房四宝［M］．北京：商务印书馆，2007.

［16］赵梦林．中国京剧脸谱［M］．北京：朝华出版社，2003.

［17］夏兰．中国戏曲文化［M］．北京：时事出版社，2007.

［18］李伟建．相声艺术教程［M］．北京：中国广播电视出版社，2020.

［19］王克瑞、杜丽华．播音员主持人训练手册（绕口令）［M］．北京：中国传媒大学出版社，2001.

［20］周维权．中国古典园林史［M］．北京：清华大学出版社，2008.